MOVIE CHARTS

A CASSELL BOOK

An Hachette Livre UK Company

First published in the UK 2009 by Cassell Illustrated,
a division of Octopus Publishing Group Ltd.
2–4 Heron Quays, London E14 4JP

Distributed in the U.S. and Canada by Octopus Books USA:
℅ Hachette Book Group USA
237 Park Avenue, New York NY 10017

A CIP catalogue record for this book is available from the
British Library.

ISBN-13: 978-1-84403-683-7

Commissioning Editor: Laura Price
Production: Caroline Alberti
Editorial Assistant: Simon Ward

Printed and bound in China

10 9 8 7 6 5 4 3 2 1

Recommended culinary accompaniments for liver in the Baltimore area

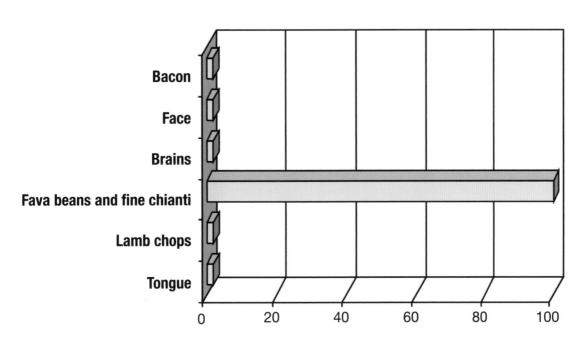

Bacon
Face
Brains
Fava beans and fine chianti
Lamb chops
Tongue

0   20   40   60   80   100

☐ Preferred accompaniment

Things we're not gonna talk about

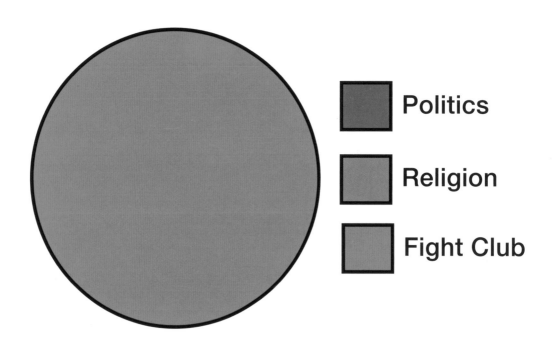

668: THE NEIGHBOR OF THE BEAST
PROPERTY COMPARISON BY LIKELIHOOD OF DEATH

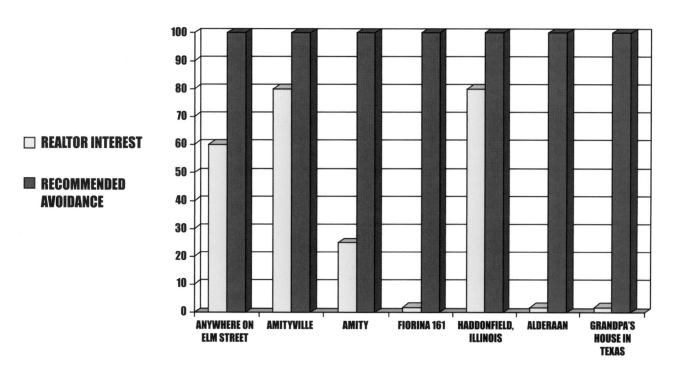

Cinematic rabbit-abuse findings

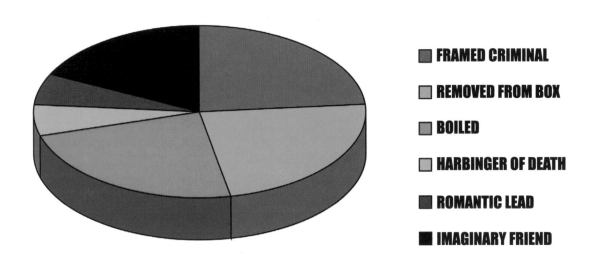

COINCIDENCE IN FACTORS AFFECTING THE CAREER ARC OF MS J FOSTER

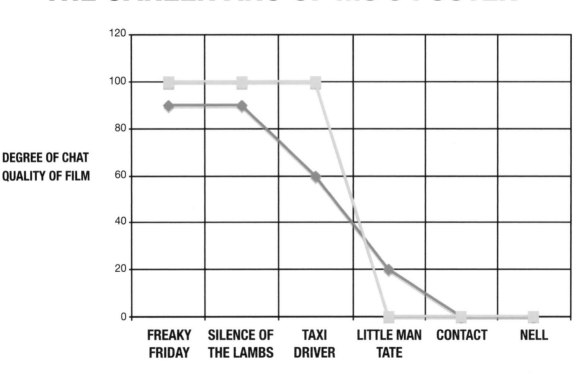

LIKELY OUTCOME OF FIRST-TIMERS TO CIRCUS MAXIMUS

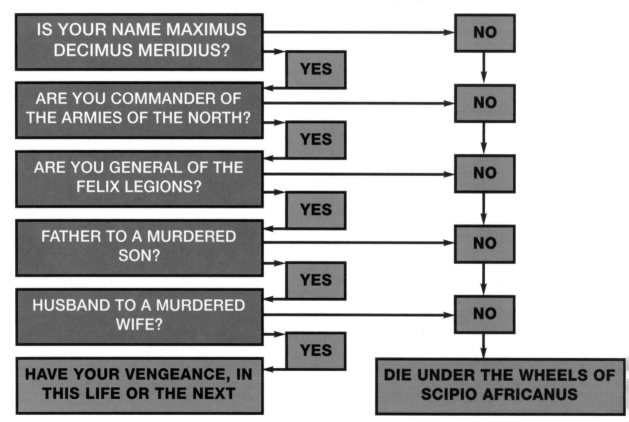

ALFRED HITCHCOCK'S BEAUTY SALON
SPRING OFFERS

SERVICES	PRICES
Ash blonde full dye	- *Free*
Honey blonde highlights	- *Free*
Platinum blonde roots	- *Free*
Strawberry blonde extension	- *Free*
Birds tangled in hair	- *3 for 1*
Showers	- *not recommended*

CASTING SUCCESSES FOR MR T. HANKS

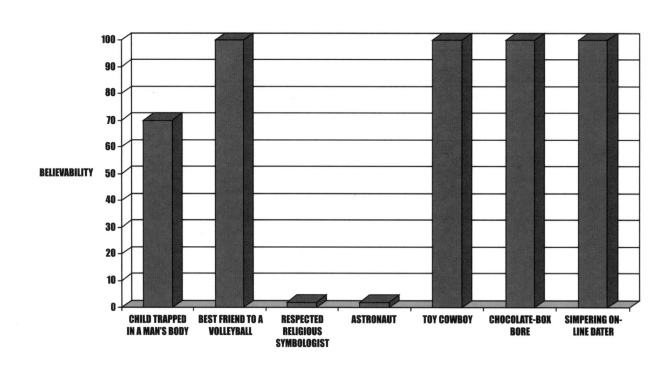

THINGS LUKE SHOULD USE

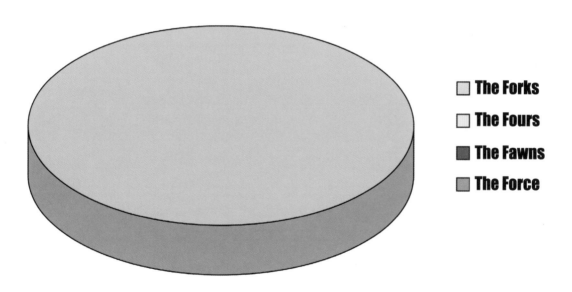

☐ The Forks
☐ The Fours
■ The Fawns
■ The Force

Likelihood of what tomorrow will be for Miss Scarlett O'Hara

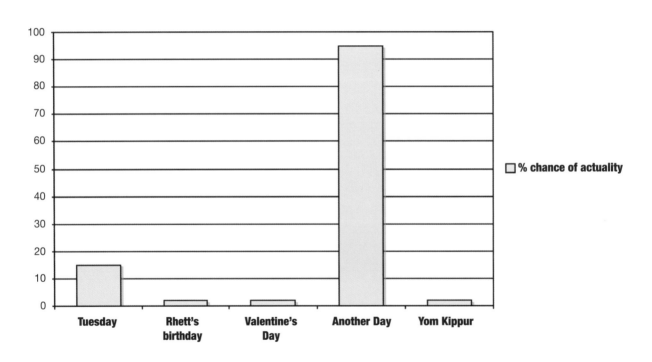

THINGS NOT TO GIVE A STRANGER IN A BAR

Your Clothes
Your Boots
Your Motorcycle
Your Sunglasses

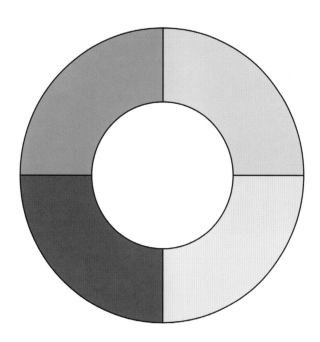

INTERNATIONAL ASSOCIATION OF ORTHODONTIC STANDARDS COMMITTEE – ACCEPTABLE QUERIES FOR PATIENTS

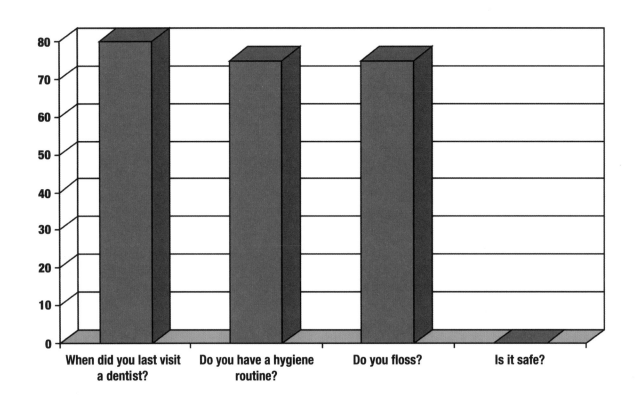

PATIENT/NURSE EXPECTATIONS OF ONGOING CARE

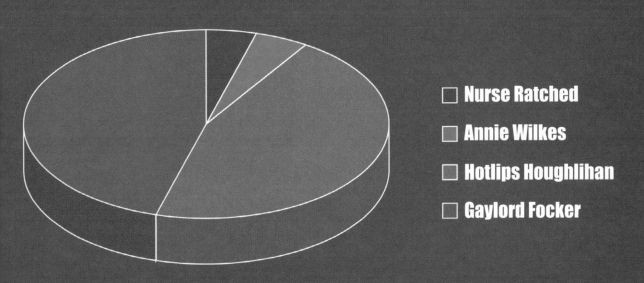

- ☐ Nurse Ratched
- ☐ Annie Wilkes
- ☐ Hotlips Houghlihan
- ☐ Gaylord Focker

DANCE AS AN EXPRESSION OF SEXUAL FRUSTRATION

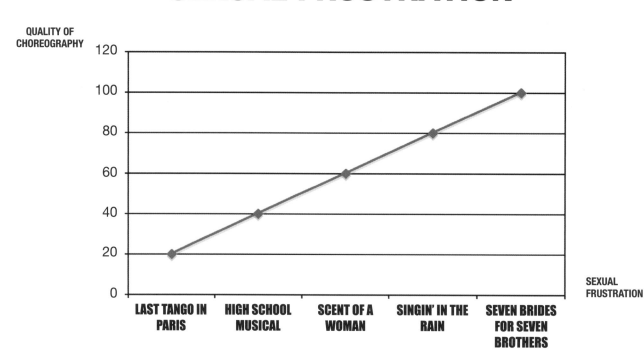

CONCERNED CITIZEN'S PHARMACEUTICAL GUIDE

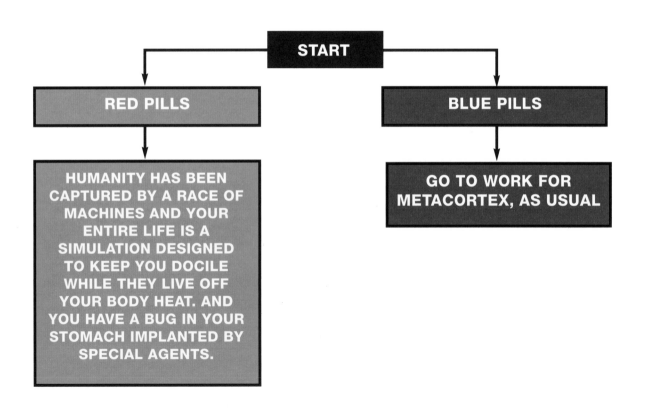

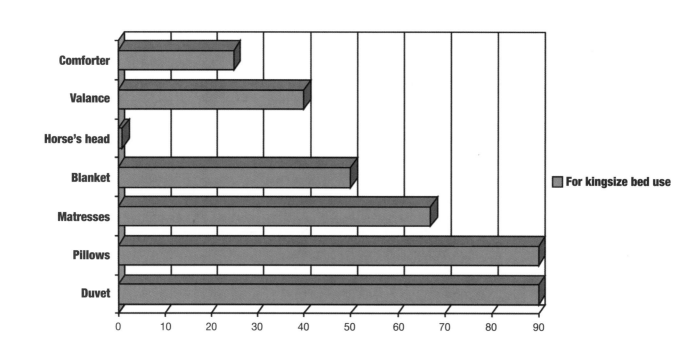

EXTENT OF DAMAGE REQUIRED DURING TURIN GOLD SHIPMENT THEFT

Predicted time of apocalypse

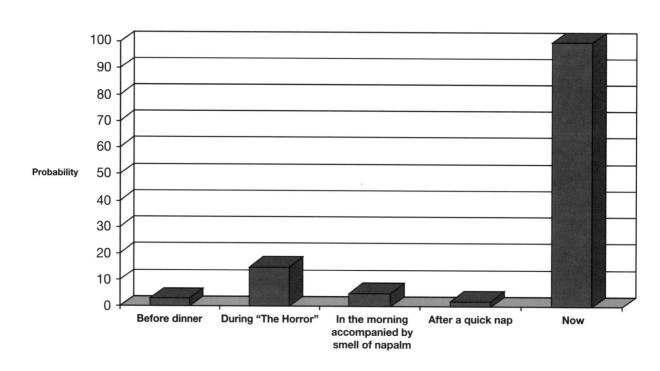

Peter Parker's journal

Monday	Tuesday	Wednesday	Thursday	Friday
Woke up, cleaned glasses. Watched Mary Jane, pined somewhat.	Uncle Ben spoke about responsibility or something.	Watched Mary Jane. Got bitten by something. Uncle Ben spoke about responsibility again. Think this is about that cup I broke.	Ate a fly. Considered spandex. Ditched glasses.	Thinking about impressing Mary Jane by becoming superhero or building a web. Bought Uncle Ben a new cup. Pizza round becoming a drag.

SOCIAL GROUPS FOR WHOM WE HAVE "COUNTRY"

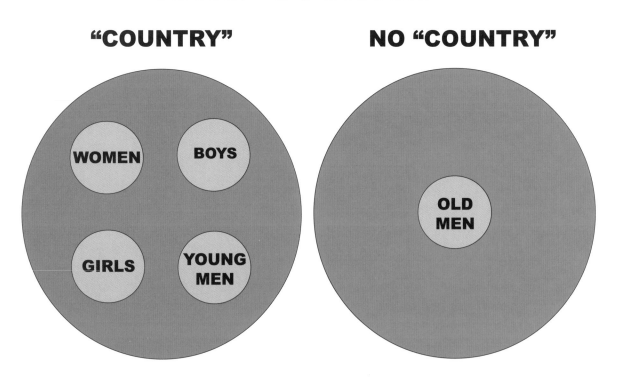

THINGS DAVE IS DOING

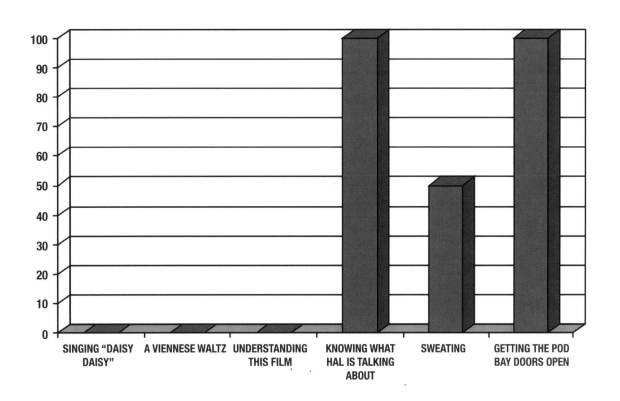

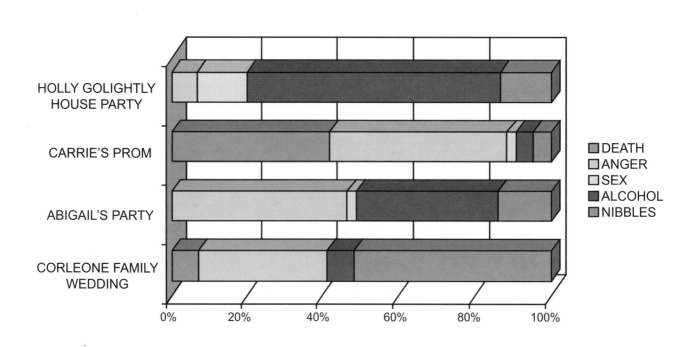

PARTY INVITE CHECK

DEATH RACE

FAST&FURIOUS

JASON STATHAM

TERMINAL ISLAND

WIN YOUR FREEDOM

CONTAINS SPOILERS

VIN DIESEL

LOS ANGELES

BRING DOWN HEROIN DEALER

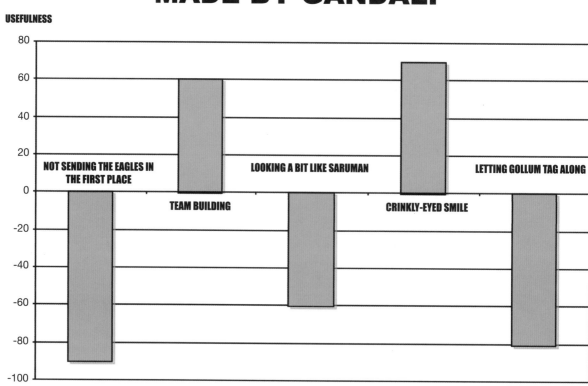

REVIEW OF MANAGERIAL CHOICES MADE BY GANDALF

GROUNDHOG DAY DAY-PLANNER

6:00 A.M.	WAKE TO "I GOT YOU BABE"	WAKE TO "I GOT YOU BABE"	WAKE TO "I GOT YOU BABE"	WAKE TO "I GOT YOU BABE"	WAKE TO "I GOT YOU BABE"
9:30 A.M.	PUNXSUTAWNEY PHIL INTERVIEW	PUNXSUTAWNEY PHIL INTERVIEW	PUNXSUTAWNEY PHIL INTERVIEW	PUNXSUTAWNEY PHIL INTERVIEW	PUNXSUTAWNEY PHIL INTERVIEW
10:00 A.M.	CHAT IN TOWN	CHAT IN TOWN	CHAT IN TOWN	CHAT IN TOWN	CHAT IN TOWN
12:00 P.M.	JAZZ PIANO LESSON	JAZZ PIANO LESSON	JAZZ PIANO LESSON	JAZZ PIANO LESSON	JAZZ PIANO LESSON
1:00 P.M.	FRENCH LESSON	FRENCH LESSON	FRENCH LESSON	FRENCH LESSON	FRENCH LESSON
2:00 P.M.	ICE SCULPTING PRACTICE	ICE SCULPTING PRACTICE	ICE SCULPTING PRACTICE	ICE SCULPTING PRACTICE	ICE SCULPTING PRACTICE
3:00 P.M.	CATCH BOY IN TREE	CATCH BOY IN TREE	CATCH BOY IN TREE	CATCH BOY IN TREE	CATCH BOY IN TREE
4:00 P.M.	FLIP CARDS INTO HAT	FLIP CARDS INTO HAT	FLIP CARDS INTO HAT	FLIP CARDS INTO HAT	FLIP CARDS INTO HAT
7:30 P.M.	PERFORM HEIMLICH MANEUVER	PERFORM HEIMLICH MANEUVER	PERFORM HEIMLICH MANEUVER	PERFORM HEIMLICH MANEUVER	PERFORM HEIMLICH MANEUVER
9:00 P.M.	HIT ON CO-ANCHOR	HIT ON CO-ANCHOR	HIT ON CO-ANCHOR	HIT ON CO-ANCHOR	HIT ON CO-ANCHOR
10:00 P.M.	BED	BED	BED	BED	BED

HOW MANY ARE ALLOWED IN THE SCOTTISH HIGHLANDS?

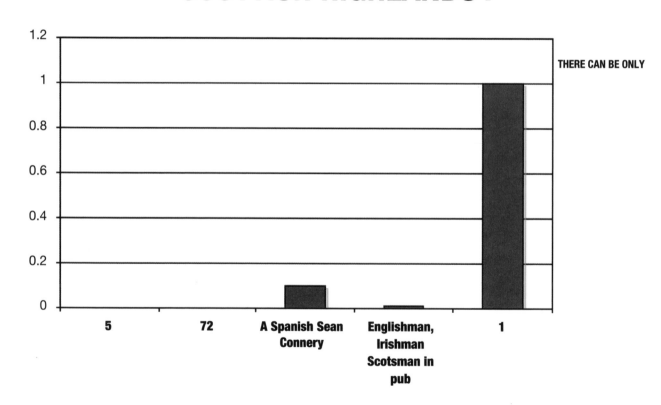

THERE CAN BE ONLY

Constituent elements of the knowledge of whistling technique

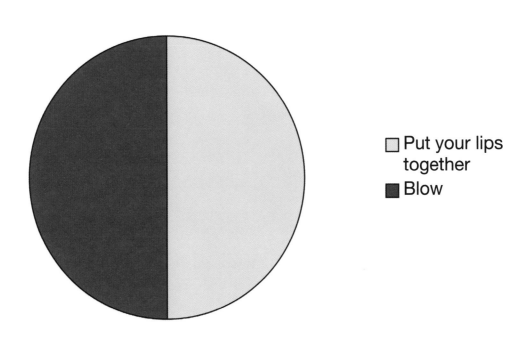

CABIN BAGGAGE PROHIBITED CHART

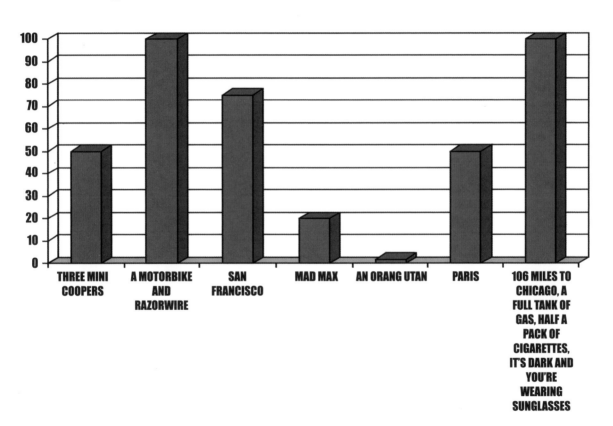

REQUIRED ELEMENTS FOR A DECENT CHASE

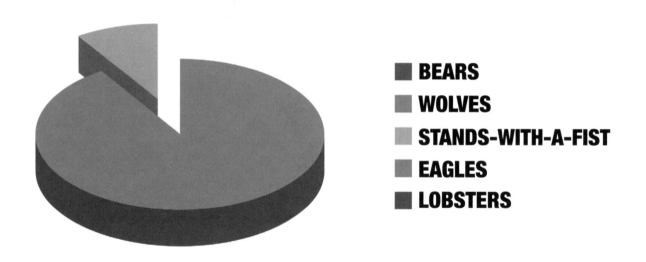

DANCING PARTNERS ON THE FRONTIER

- BEARS
- WOLVES
- STANDS-WITH-A-FIST
- EAGLES
- LOBSTERS

WATERFRONT BUM CENSUS

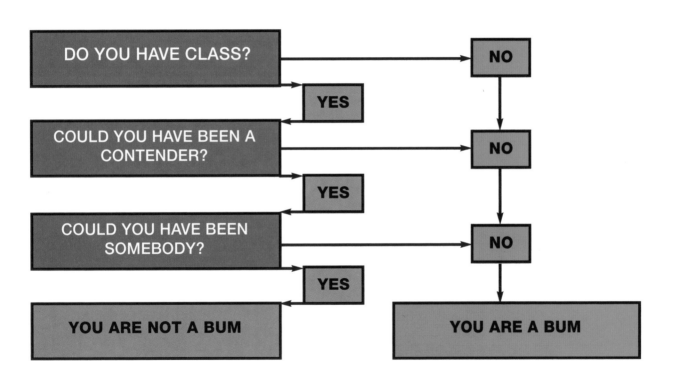

2009 ACCOMMODATION GUIDE
TO MOVIE HOTELS

OVERLOOK HOTEL, COLORADO, USA	☆ ☆ ☆ ☆ ☆
BATES MOTEL, ARIZONA, USA	☆ ☆ ☆ ☆ ☆
CALIFORNIA SUITE, CALIFORNIA, USA	★ ★ ★ ★ ★
SABENA HOTEL DOS MILLE CALINES, KIGALE, RWANDA	☆ ☆ ☆ ☆ ☆
ROOM 1408, DOLPHIN HOTEL, NY, NY, USA	☆ ☆ ☆ ☆ ☆
THE HOSTEL, BRATISLAVA, SLOVAKIA	☆ ☆ ☆ ☆ ☆

PEOPLE YOU'RE TALKIN' TO

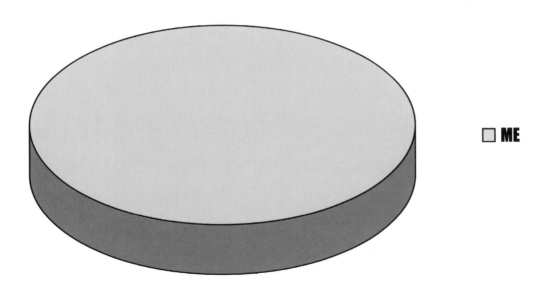

☐ ME

SOUTHERN PACIFIC RAILROADS
ARIZONA TIMETABLE

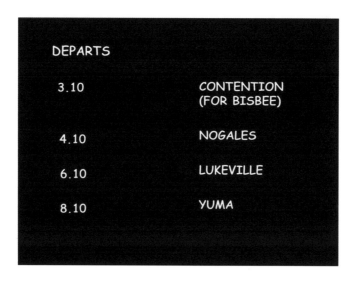

DEPARTS	
3.10	CONTENTION (FOR BISBEE)
4.10	NOGALES
6.10	LUKEVILLE
8.10	YUMA

COINCIDENCE IN FACTORS AFFECTING THE CAREER ARC OF MR J TRAVOLTA

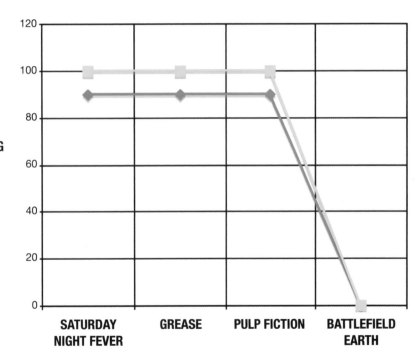

THINGS A FEW GOOD MEN CAN'T HANDLE

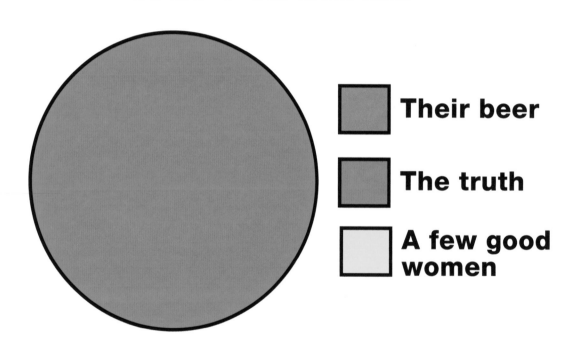

DEGREE OF SOMNOLENCE BY TITLE

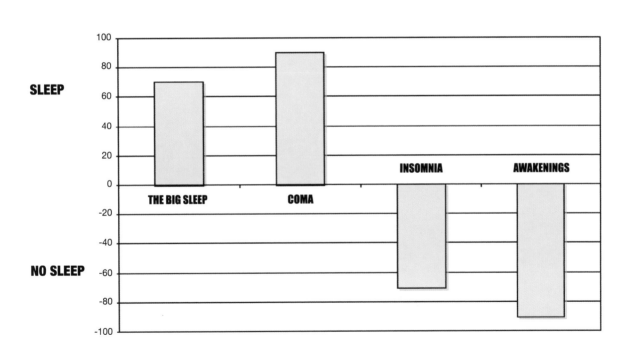

72-HOUR FORECAST
NEW YORK CITY

TODAY

TOMORROW

THE DAY AFTER TOMORROW

TSUNAMI & ICE STORM (WITH WOLVES)

EXPECTATIONS OF MR AURIC GOLDFINGER REGARDING MR JAMES BOND

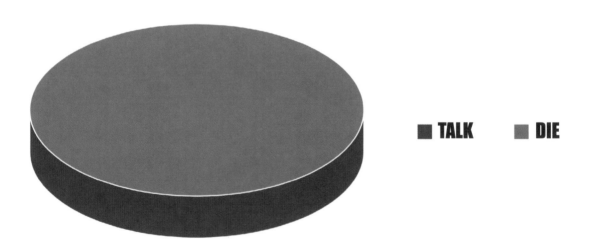

TALK   DIE

MOST COMMON ROUTES TO LIFE ON A DESERT ISLAND

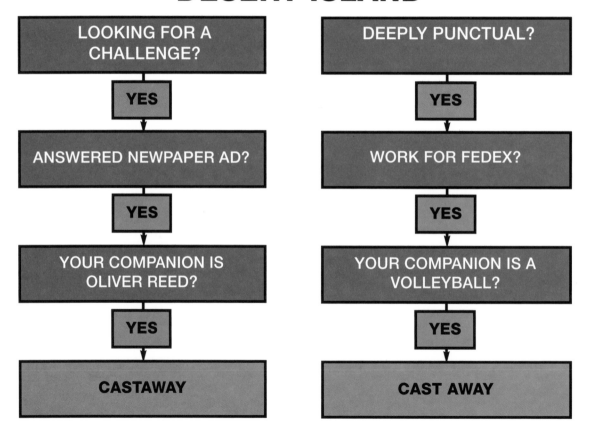

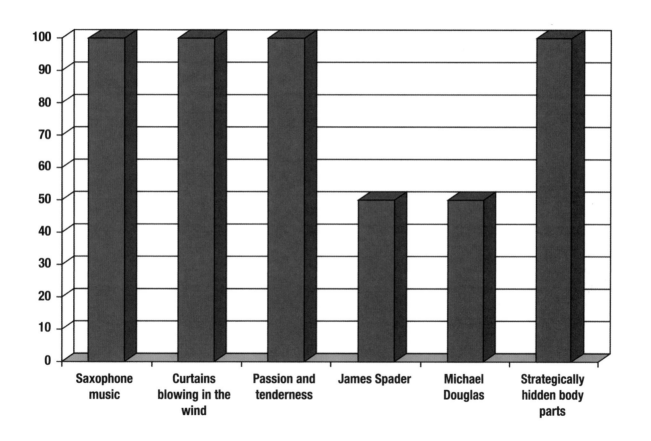

REQUIRED ELEMENTS IN A SEX SCENE

Things they've seen you wouldn't believe

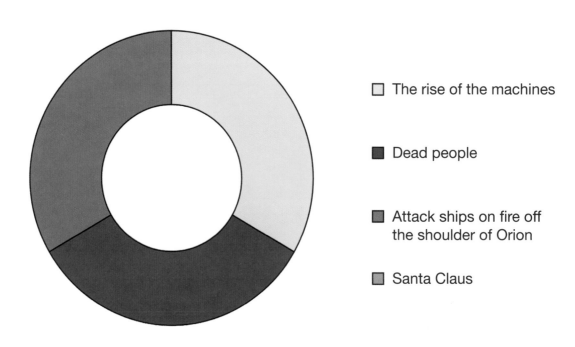

- ☐ The rise of the machines
- ☐ Dead people
- ☐ Attack ships on fire off the shoulder of Orion
- ☐ Santa Claus

DEGREE OF BLAXPLOITATION IN 1970s CINEMA

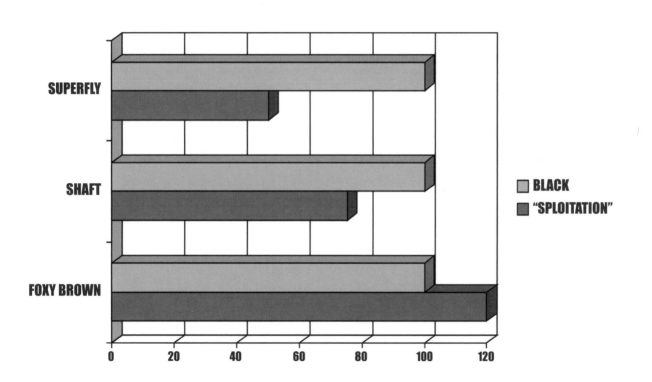

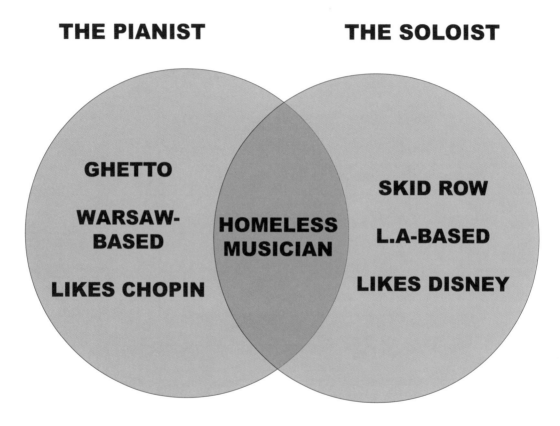

THE PIANIST

THE SOLOIST

GHETTO

WARSAW-BASED

LIKES CHOPIN

HOMELESS MUSICIAN

SKID ROW

L.A-BASED

LIKES DISNEY

RELATIVE REFUSABILITY OF MOVIE MADE MEN

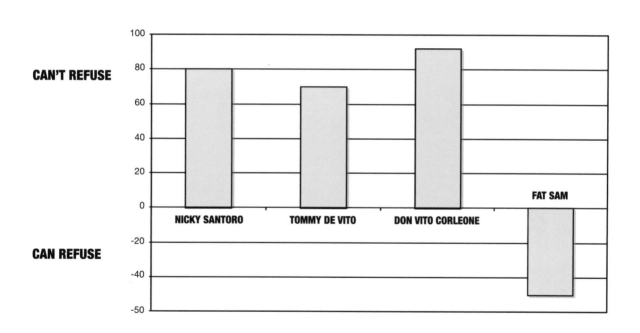

MITCH AND MURRAY
PROFIT & LOSS, 1992

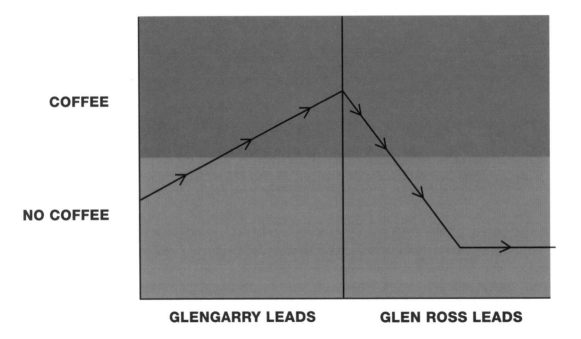

WILD-ONE JOHNNY'S CHECKLIST OF THINGS TO REBEL AGAINST

☐ THE KOREAN WAR

☐ THE HOUSE COMMITTEE ON UN-AMERICAN ACTIVITIES

☐ THE EXECUTION OF THE ROSENBERGS

☐ THE SUPRESSION OF THE MAU MAUS

☒ WHATEVER KATHIE BLEEKER HAS GOT

☐ THE H BOMB

LOGAN'S MIDLIFE CRISIS SIGNS

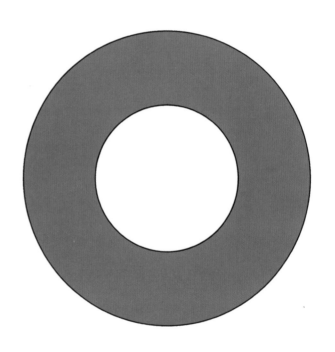

☐ GREY HAIR

☐ ACHING JOINTS

■ DESIRE FOR SPORTS CAR

■ FLASHING RED PALM

ALEXANDRIA BEVERAGE SERVING GUIDE

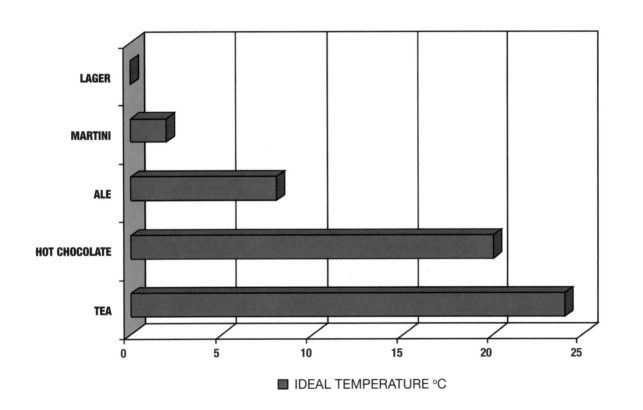

IDEAL TEMPERATURE °C

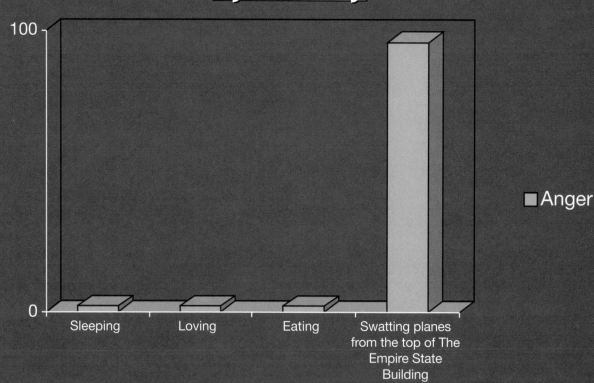

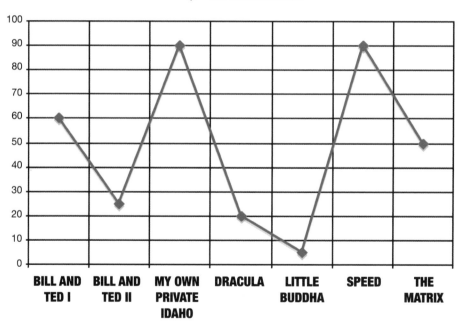

KEANU REEVES EXPRESSIVENESS BY MOVIE

◆ EXPRESSIVENESS

ROGER MOORE LINE

◆ EXPRESSIVENESS

ROGER MOORE LINE

53

I SEE...

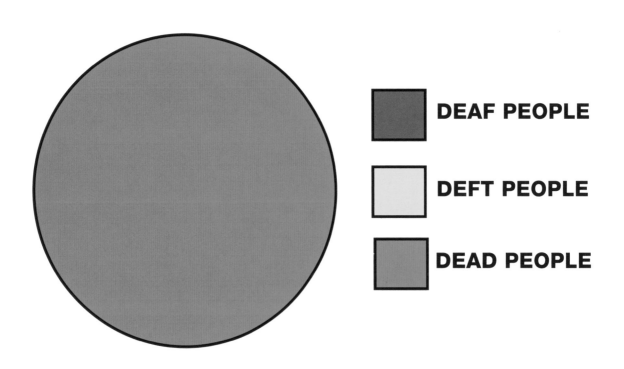

Follicular assessment of the career of Mr B Willis

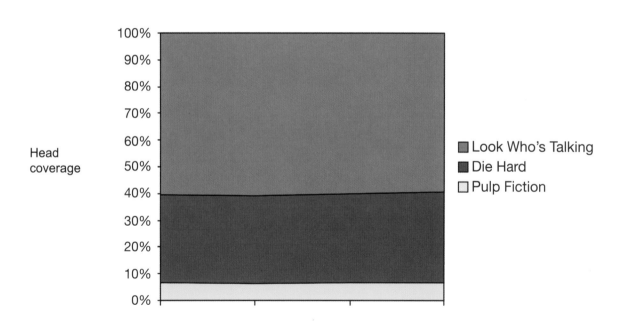

Mr Al Pacino's levels of shoutiness

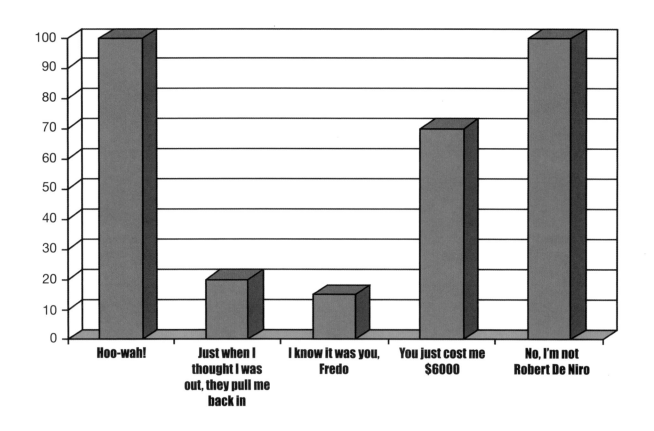

QUESTIONS REGARDING THE LAST KNOWN ACTIONS OF MRS WAYNE (DECEASED)

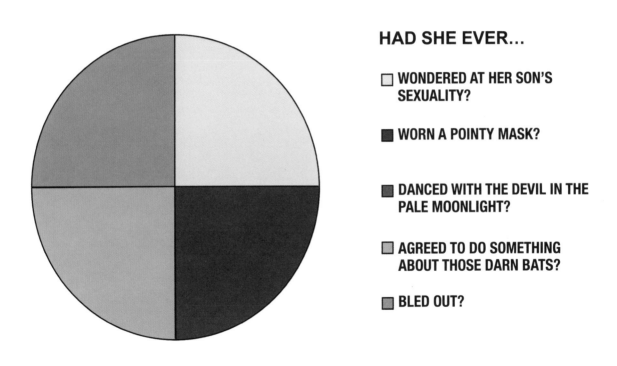

HAD SHE EVER...

☐ WONDERED AT HER SON'S SEXUALITY?

■ WORN A POINTY MASK?

■ DANCED WITH THE DEVIL IN THE PALE MOONLIGHT?

■ AGREED TO DO SOMETHING ABOUT THOSE DARN BATS?

■ BLED OUT?

COMPARATIVE DESIRABLILITY OF LIEUTENANTS – BY TASK

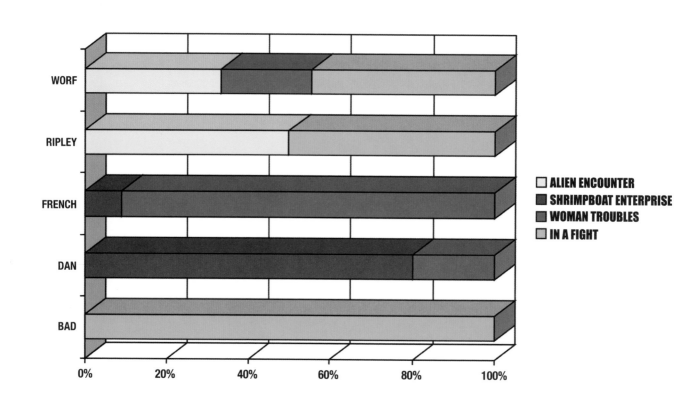

CARTOON CROW EXPERIENCE CHECKLIST

- ☒ SAW A PEANUT STAND
- ☒ HEARD A RUBBER BAND
- ☒ SAW A FRONT PORCH SWING
- ☒ HEARD A DIAMOND RING
- ☒ HEARD A FIRESIDE CHAT
- ☒ SAW A BASEBALL BAT
- ☐ SAW AN ELEPHANT FLY

EXPECTATIONS OF CLEANLINESS BY SIZE OF GROUP

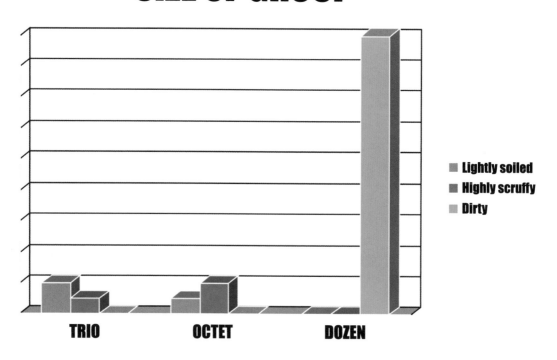

COMPARATIVE NUMBERS OF
DEAD MEN WALKING

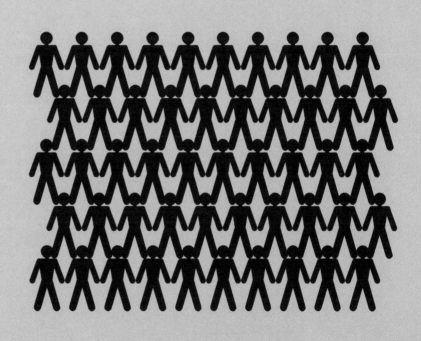

RECOMMENDED BODIES WITH WHOM TO SHARE A PROBLEM

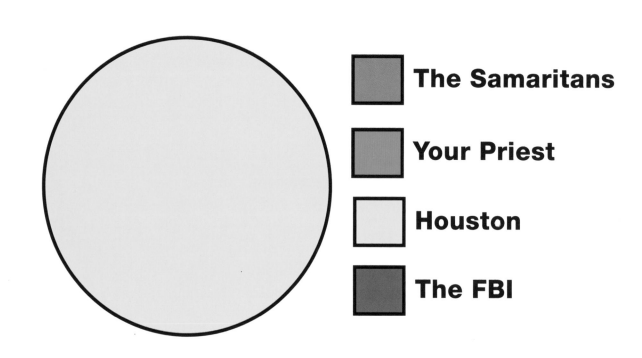

THE ANSWERS THE SLAVES REALLY WANTED TO GIVE

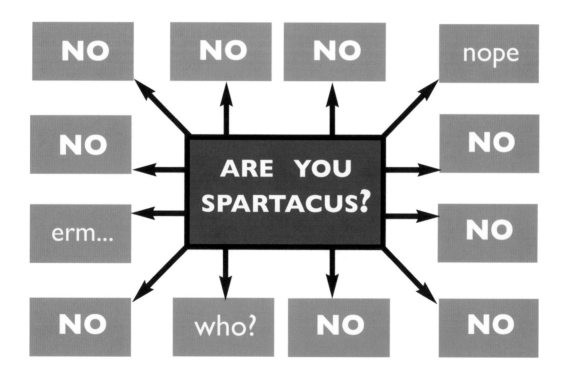

FLOWCHART DETERMINING OUTCOME OF A MATTER:

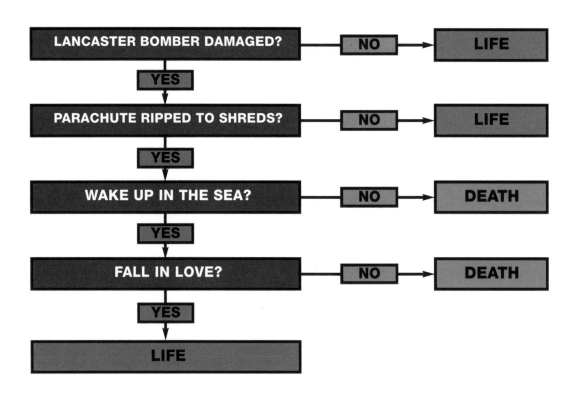

Major factors affecting the distribution of industry awards

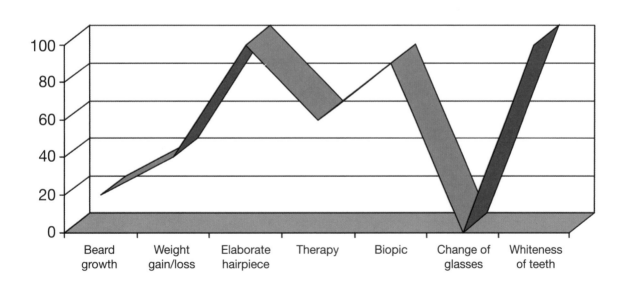

ITEMS NEEDED FOR SUCCESSFUL
JULY 4th WEEKEND IN AMITY

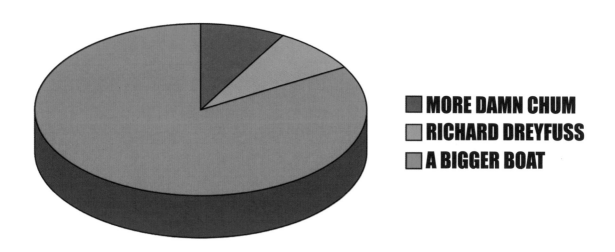

COMPARATIVE EFFECT OF EMOTIONAL PEAKS IN ANIMATED FILMS

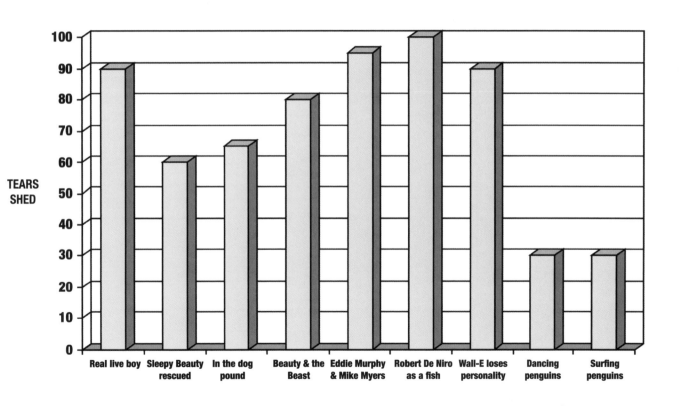

Average width of John Wayne's gait by career highlight

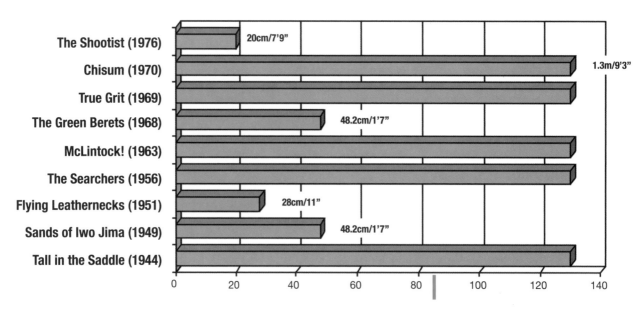

Av = 88.2cm/2'11"
(All measurements from outer edge of foot.)

Things Rose won't let go of after Titanic sinks

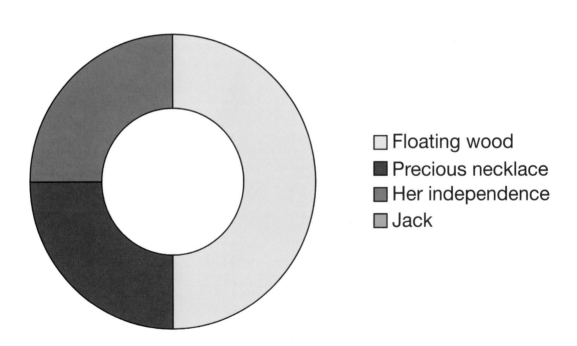

- ☐ Floating wood
- ■ Precious necklace
- ▨ Her independence
- ☐ Jack

THE BREAKFAST-MOVIE FOOD PYRAMID SHOWING RELATIVE NUTRITIONAL VALUES

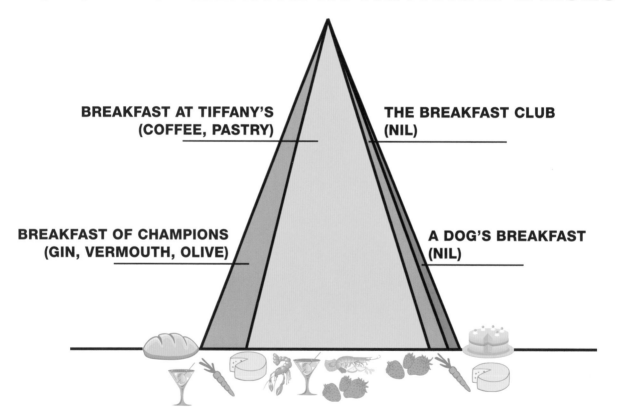

BREAKFAST AT TIFFANY'S
(COFFEE, PASTRY)

THE BREAKFAST CLUB
(NIL)

BREAKFAST OF CHAMPIONS
(GIN, VERMOUTH, OLIVE)

A DOG'S BREAKFAST
(NIL)

SUSPECT DESCRIPTION – FARGO DIVISION

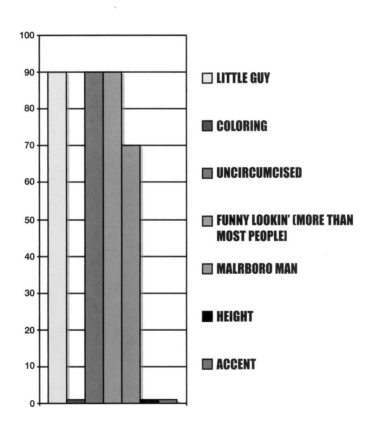

STAR COMMAND STANDARD-ISSUE GAZETTEER

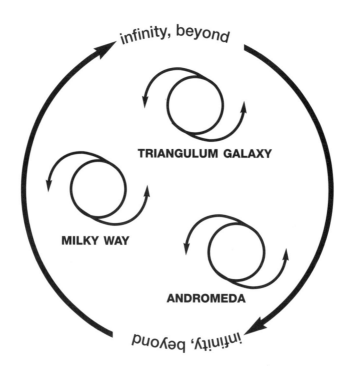

MOVIES WITH PETS: WATCHABILITY OVER TIME

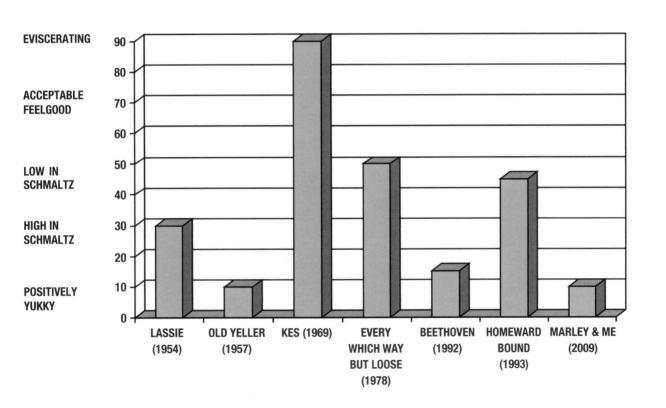

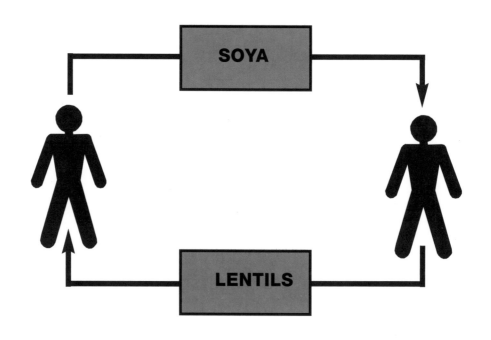

SOYLENT GREEN FOOD CHAIN

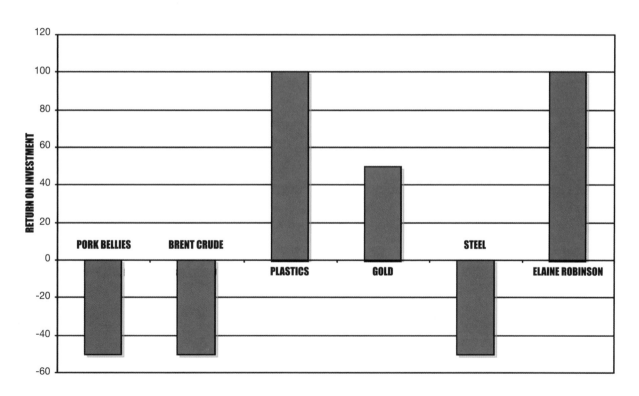

BENJAMIN BRADDOCK'S INVESTMENT PORTFOLIO

ADDICTION ANALYSIS
BY PROTAGONIST

	ALCOHOL	TOBACCO	NITROUS OXIDE	MARI-JUANA	MAGIC FEATHER	HEROIN
FRANK BOOTH			✔			
MARK RENTON						✔
PHILIP MARLOWE	✔	✔				
DUMBO					✔	
JEFFREY LEBOWSKI				✔		
FRANKIE MACHINE						✔

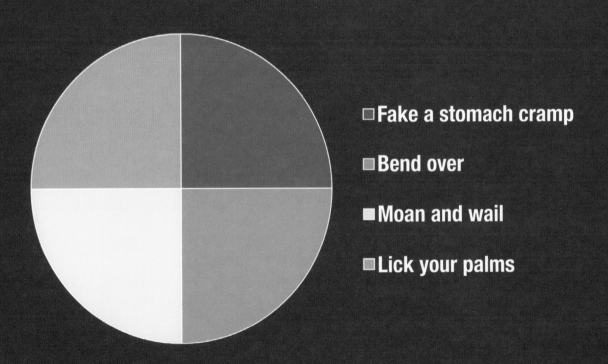

MASTER BUELLER'S KEY TO FAKING OUT THE PARENTS

- Fake a stomach cramp
- Bend over
- Moan and wail
- Lick your palms

DEGREE OF BIZARRENESS OF MONSTER

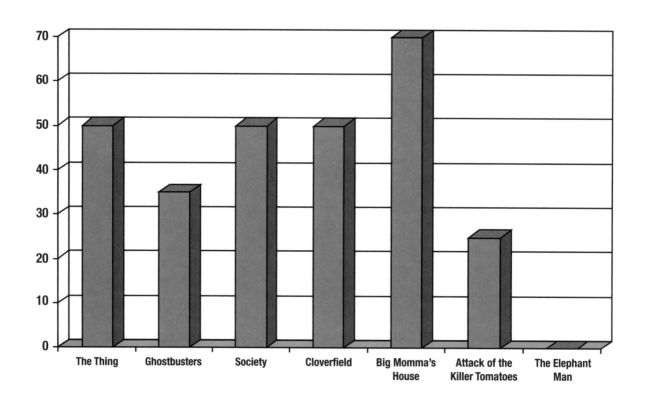

MOVIE GUILT GUIDE

TWELVE ANGRY MEN

THE KID
DIDN'T DO IT.

TWELVE MONKEYS

"WE DID IT."

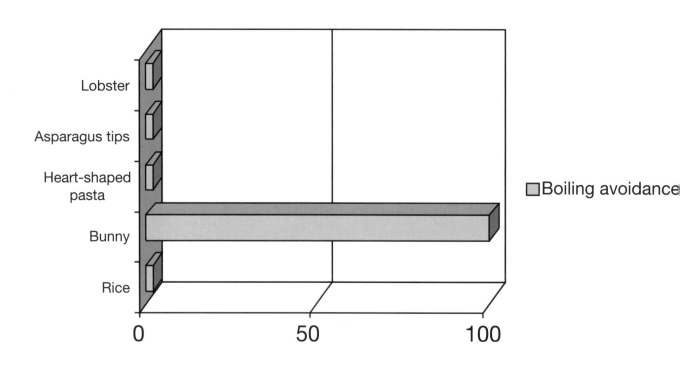

Items to avoid boiling during romance

Boiling avoidance

Nationality of werewolves in London

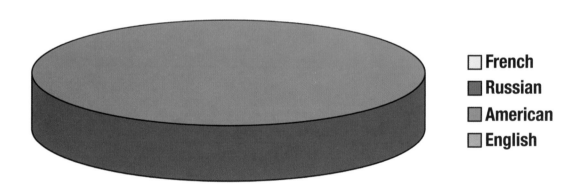

☐ French
■ Russian
▨ American
▨ English

DEGREES OF DUDITY

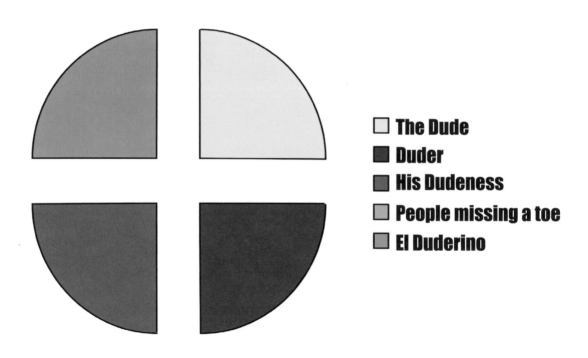

COMPARATIVE DESIRABLILITY OF CRAFT – BY TASK

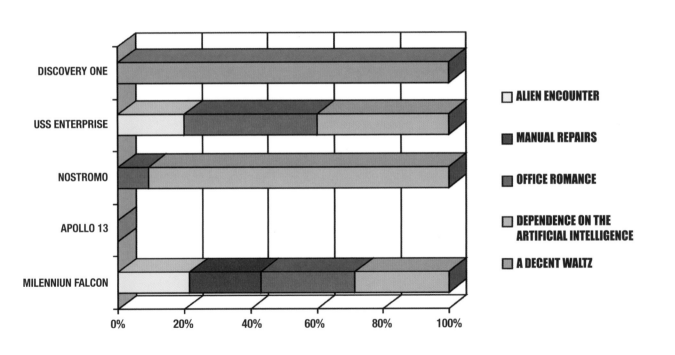

TITTY TWISTER DRINKS MENU

CERVEZA	$2.00
TEQUILA	$2.00
MARGARITA	$3.00
BLOOD	$-

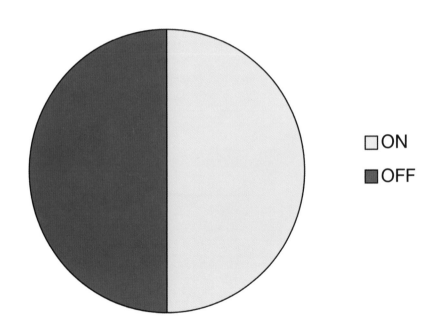

ANCIENT MIYAGI WAX TECHNIQUE

□ ON
■ OFF

DECLINING ONE-LINER QUOTIENT BETWEEN ARNIE PROMISING TO RETURN AND ACTUALLY RETURNING

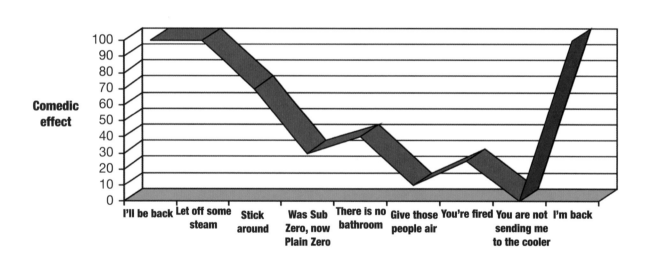

MARK RENTON'S THINGS TO CHOOSE FROM

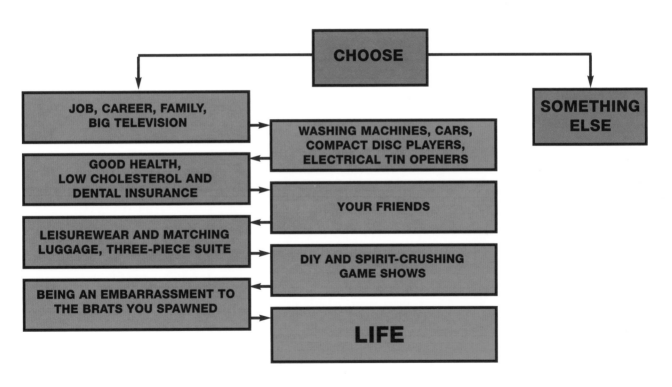

PEOPLE WHO CAN PUT BABY IN THE CORNER

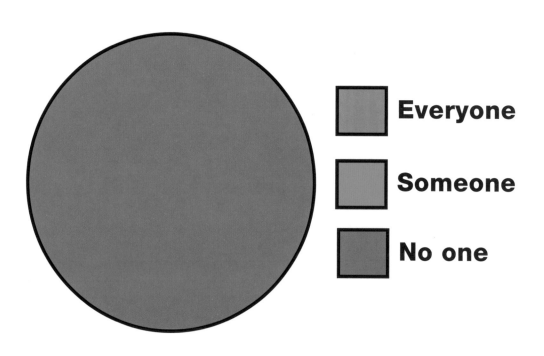

CRIME BOSS JOE CABOT'S TIMESHEET FOR EMPLOYEES GOING TO WORK

NAME	MR WHITE	MR BLOND	MR BROWN	MR PINK	MR ORANGE	MR YELLOW	MR BLUE	MR BEIGE	MR B. RACING-GREEN
A.M.	✔	✔	✔	✔	✔	✗	✔	✗	✗
LUNCH									
P.M.	✔	✔	(ABSENT)	✔	(ABSENT)	✗	✔	✗	✗

THINGS WE DON'T NEED

STINKIN' BADGES

STINKING BADGERS

TREASURE OF THE SIERRA MADRE

THE WIND IN THE WILLOWS

CIRCUIT DIAGRAM FOR GUITAR-AMPLIFIER CAPACITOR

$V=11$

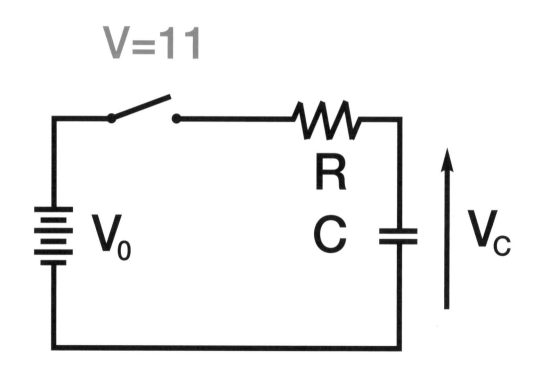

DIRTY HARRY'S ONE QUESTION FOR OTHERS TO ASK THEMSELVES

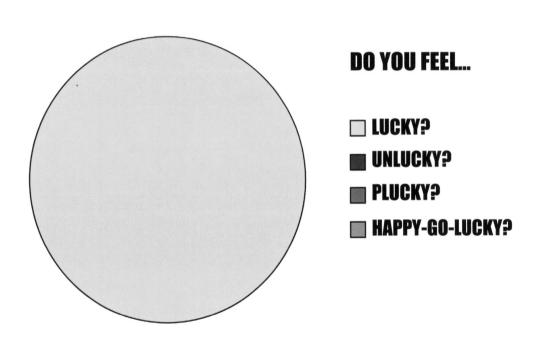

DO YOU FEEL...

- ☐ LUCKY?
- ■ UNLUCKY?
- ■ PLUCKY?
- ■ HAPPY-GO-LUCKY?

Leonard Shelby's priorities in Memento

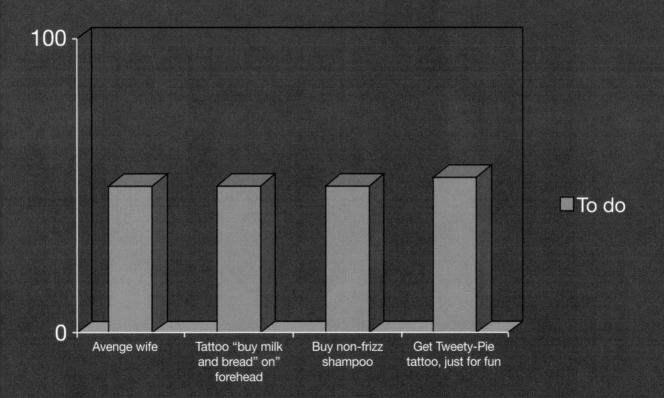

RELATIVE LETHALITIES OF FEMMES FATALES

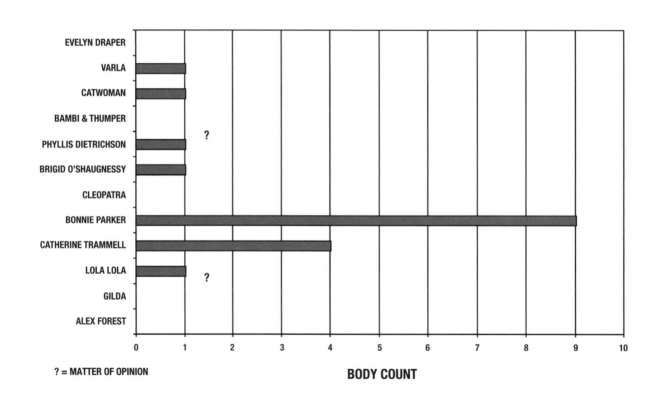

? = MATTER OF OPINION

BODY COUNT

MOVIE WINE GUIDE

SIDEWAYS

WITHNAIL & I

CALIFORNIA
WINES

THE FINEST
WINES
AVAILABLE TO
HUMANITY

ANSWERS

3. The Silence of the Lambs
4. Fight Club
5. A Nightmare on Elm Street; The Amityville Horror; Jaws; Alien 3; Halloween; Star Wars: Episode IV – A New Hope; The Texas Chainsaw Massacre
6. Who Framed Roger Rabbit?; Con Air; Fatal Attraction; Donnie Darko; Who Framed Roger Rabbit?; Harvey
7. Jodie Foster's career – by chat
8. Gladiator
9. Alfred Hitchcock films: Marnie; The Birds; Psycho
10. Big; Cast Away; The Da Vinci Code; Apollo 13, Toy Story; Forrest Gump; You've Got Mail
11. Star Wars: Episode IV – A New Hope
12. Gone With the Wind
13. Terminator
14. Marathon Man
15. One Flew Over the Cuckoo's Nest; Misery; "M*A*S*H"; Meet the Fockers
16. Sexual Frustration
17. The Matrix
18. The Godfather
19. The Italian Job
20. Apocalypse Now
21. Spider-man
22. No Country for Old Men
23. 2001: A Space Odyssey
24. Breakfast at Tiffany's; Carrie; Abigail's Party; The Godfather
25. Death Race; Fast & Furious
26. Lord of the Rings trilogy
27. Groundhog Day
28. Highlander
29. To Have and Have Not
30. Snakes on a Plane
31. The Italian Job; The Great Escape; Bullitt; Mad Max; Every Which Way But Loose; The French Connection; The Blues Brothers

32. Dances With Wolves
33. On The Waterfront
34. The Shining; Psycho; California Suite; Hotel Rwanda; 1408; Hostel
35. Taxi Driver
36. 3.10 to Yuma
37. John Travolta's career – by dance
38. A Few Good Men
39. Somnolence
40. The Day After Tomorrow
41. Goldfinger
42. Castaway; Cast Away
43. Sex scenes
44. Terminator; The Sixth Sense; Blade Runner; Miracle on 34th Street
45. Blaxploitation
46. The Pianist; The Soloist
47. Casino; GoodFellas; The Godfather, Bugsy Malone
48. Glengarry Glen Ross
49. The Wild One
50. Logan's Run
51. Ice Cold in Alex
52. King Kong
53. Keanu Reeves' Movies
54. Sixth Sense
55. Bruce Willis' career – by hair length
56. Scent of a Woman; The Godfather: Part III; The Godfather: Part II; Glengarry Glen Ross
57. Batman
58. Star Trek; Alien; The French Lieutenant's Woman; Forest Gump; Bad Lieutenant
59. Dumbo
60. The Dirty Dozen
61. Dead Man Walking; Fifty Dead Men Walking
62. Apollo 13
63. Spartacus
64. A Matter of Life and Death/Stairway to Heaven (US)
65. Industry awards
66. Jaws

67. Pinocchio; Sleeping Beauty; The Lady and the Tramp; Beauty and the Beast; Shrek; Shark Tale; WALL-E; Happy Feet; Surf's Up
68. John Wayne's career – by gait
69. Titanic
70. Breakfasts by movie
71. Fargo
72. Toy Story
73. Pet Movies
74. Soylent Green
75. The Graduate
76. Blue Velvet; Trainspotting; The Big Sleep; Dumbo; The Big Lebowski; The Man with the Golden Arm
77. Ferris Bueller's Day Off
78. Bizarreness of Monster
79. Twelve Angry Men; Twelve Monkeys
80. Fatal Attraction
81. American Werewolf in London
82. The Big Lebowski
83. 2001: A Space Odyssey; Star Trek; Alien; Apollo 13; Star Wars
84. From Dusk Til Dawn
85. The Karate Kid
86. Terminator; Commando, Predator; Running Man; Kindergarten Cop; Total Recall; True Lies; Batman and Robin; Terminator 3
87. Trainspotting
88. Dirty Dancing
89. Reservoir Dogs
90. Treasure of the Sierra Madre; Wind in the Willows
91. This is Spinal Tap
92. Dirty Harry
93. Memento
94. Play Misty for Me; Faster, Pussycat! Kill! Kill!; Catwoman; Diamonds are Forever; Double Indemnity; The Maltese Falcon; Cleopatra; Bonnie and Clyde; Basic Instinct; Lolita; Gilda; Fatal Attraction
95. Sideways; Withnail & I